Sources of
Law, Legal Change,
and
Ambiguity

Alan Watson

UNIVERSITY OF PENNSYLVANIA PRESS
Philadelphia

Designed by Design for Publishing, Bob Nance

Copyright © 1984 by the
University of Pennsylvania Press

Library of Congress Cataloging in Publication Data

Watson, Alan.
  Sources of law, legal change, and ambiguity.

  Includes index.
  1. Law—Sources. 2. Law reform. 3. Law—History and
criticism. I. Title.
K280.W37 1984   340   83-21783
ISBN 0-8122-7919-0

Printed in the United States of America

for Carleton B. Chapman

Contents

Acknowledgments

The Biddle Law Library of the University of Pennsylvania provided me with many of the volumes needed for this study, but a Fellowship from the American Bar Foundation enabled me to pursue my researches abroad, notably at the Max-Planck Institut für europäische Rechtsgeschichte in Frankfurt, the National Library of Scotland in Edinburgh, and the Law Library of the University of Oxford. To the members of all these institutions I express my gratitude, as well as to my friends, John Barton, Robert Black, Michael Hoeflich, Neil MacCormick, Maria Smolka, Wolfgang Wagner and Armin Wolf, who read all or most of the book in typescript and were generous with helpful criticism. For the errors that remain I wish to plead the second defence of Sir George Mackenzie in the Advertisement to the second edition of *The Institutions of the Law of Scotland* (1688). Chapter 6, "Two-Tier Law," with minor alterations, formed the first part of an article of the same name originally published in the *International and Comparative Law Quarterly*, 27 (1978), 552ff. I am grateful to the editors for their permission to republish it here.

Many of the works used for this study are not easily accessible, hence to show the evidence on which I base my argument I have often preferred to quote at length rather than paraphrase. For the same reason I usually reproduce the original in addition to giving my own translation into English.

Abbreviations

C.	*Codex Justiniani*
C. Th.	*Codex Theodosiani*
D.	*Digesta Justiniani*
G.	*Gai Institutiones*
h. t.	The same Title of Justinian's, *Digest* as the previously cited text.
J.	*Justiniani Institutiones*
Jolowicz & Nicholas, *Historical Introduction*	H. F. Jolowicz & B. Nicholas, *Historical Introduction to the Study of Roman Law,* 3d ed. (Cambridge: Cambridge University Press, 1972)
Kaser, R. Pr. 1, 2	M. Kaser, *Das römische Privatrecht* 2d ed., vol. 1 (Munich: Beck, 1971); vol. 2 (1975)
L.Q.R.	*Law Quarterly Review*
Nov.	*Novellae Justiniani*
Thomas, *Textbook*	J.A.C. Thomas, *Textbook of Roman Law* (Amsterdam: North Holland, 1976)

T.V.R.	*Tijdschrift voor Rechtsgeschiedenis*
Watson, *Making of the Civil Law*	Alan Watson, *The Making of the Civil Law* (Cambridge, Mass.: Harvard University Press, 1981)

Introduction

Humans are social animals, and various mechanisms, such as religion, accepted standards of ethical behavior, and good manners, have developed to enable them to live (relatively) peacefully in society. Law is one such mechanism, and its distinguishing feature, I believe, is the availability of a process which has the necessary function of inhibiting further unregulated conflict by means of a decision. Within the context of the process law has two necessary roles: a claim of legal right or power is needed to call the process into being, and law is used to validate the decision. To fulfill these functions, law, whether it is regarded as already existing and simply to be discovered, or made by preceding conscious human determination, or to be made during the instant case, has to achieve some express linguistic formulation. And the formulation to have effect must contain within it, at least implicitly, the seeds of legitimacy.

The formulation is authoritative when it is treated by the courts as resting on a basis which the courts habitually regard as determinative for their decisions. Such bases differ from time to time and from place to place, and in developed Western societies they have been at times custom, legislation, juristic opinion, and preceding judicial decision. These bases are all included within the notion of "sources of law," and for convenience "sources of law" is the term that will be used for them. The term "sources of law" is notoriously ambiguous, and it will be used here only with regard to these four bases of legal legitimacy. The term will not be used of, say, prevailing moral values or economic conditions that influence the content of a new legal rule, or of what is termed "natural law," except insofar as relatively articulate "natural law" doctrines have been regarded by courts as determinative for their decisions. The term also is always used here within a particular historical framework. When I discuss custom, for example, I am concerned not with the general phenomenon of custom as a means of legal development or its average satisfactoriness as such a means, but custom as courts used it to ground their decisions in a particular societal context such as thirteenth-century France. In addition, I use the term "source of law" with a concrete rather than abstract meaning. When, for instance, I claim that legislation proved unsatisfactory for lawmaking in England in the first half of this century, I do not refer to legislation in the general sense of a formal promulgation of an act by a legislature, but mean to embrace the entire legislative process as it worked at that place and time. It is in this sense that one can ascribe defects in the content or clarity of the law directly to the source of law.

My aim is to set out the sources of law as they have been used, understood, and interpreted at various times and places within the Western legal tradition, not for purposes of description, but to indicate that there has often been profound indifference among the influential members of the legal community who had some power to change the law as to the quality of these sources and their fitness both for developing the law and for clarifying ambiguities. The significance of this indifference is greatly increased if one accepts, as I would accept, that the nature of the available sources of law has a powerful impact on legal change. The claim, of course, is not that everyone everywhere has always partaken of this indifference, only that for considerable stretches of time the indifference has led to an ignoring of, and lack of comment on, obvious defects, and has been at least great enough to prevent clearly needed reforms. The indifference is the more striking when it can be demonstrated, as often, that the poor quality of the existing sources was recognized, but changes were not forthcoming for a very long time. The phenomenon of, at best, mediocre sources of law occurred, I want to show, throughout most of the history of Roman law before Justinian; in Germany and France from the thirteenth to the fifteenth centuries; and in Europe in general after the reception of

Roman law but before the modern movement for codification proved overwhelming; and it still occurs, despite some recent improvements, in modern England. These places and times are chosen as examples. Such a widespread and enduring phenomenon should not be ignored. The mediocrity of the sources, and the possibility of improvement, has to be judged, of course, by conditions at the time, not those prevailing today.

The book accordingly has a wide sweep. What is a source of law at one time and place will not always have that role elsewhere and at a different time. Statute was a source of private law in ancient Rome but could scarcely be used for that purpose in Germany or France between the thirteenth and fifteenth centuries—a period studied here—because of prevailing political conditions. Conversely, custom was the most fruitful source of law for Germany and France for the times just mentioned, but the prevalence of powerful juristic doctrine and imperial rescripts left virtually no scope for custom to make law in the early Roman empire. Again, all lawmaking or lawfinding rests ultimately on a theory of the nature of law even if that theory is implicit and even if that theory is not articulately present in the consciousness of the lawmaker or lawfinder. And such theories have been different at different times and at different places. Despite this, the theme of the book is unitary. It deals with what those people who were involved with the law at the particular time and in the particular place considered as formulations containing seeds of legitimacy: the ease or difficulty that they experienced both in determining what the law was and in developing new law.

To illustrate the point about the way in which legal theories can be implicit in attitudes to legal processes and sources of law: one might suggest that at some times and in some political circumstances a voluntaristic attitude prevails, as manifested in the belief that the content of legal rules is determined or determinable by the will of a lawgiver or lawmaker, whether legislator or judge. Where this is so, the "sources of law" are also in their very nature processes of formulation of rules in relatively explicit form, though, as the modern English conception of precedent as a form of "judge-made law" shows, such formulations can be remarkably unclear (see chapter 4 below). At other times and in other places, often characterized by the absence of centralized political authority or at least of constancy of legislative policy where centralized authorities exist, nonvoluntaristic legal theories have tended to prevail. In such contexts, the legitimacy of legal decisions is grounded in "natural law," or "custom," or on both together, settled custom being taken (as by Stair in seventeenth-century Scotland) to be evidentiary of "the law of nature and reason." Where this view is prevalent, there is a noticeable tension, rather than identity, as between the "source of law" and the actual formulation of the law. Here the problem of "sources" in our sense becomes a problem about securing satisfactory formulations of norms of behavior whose appropriateness as norms does not derive from *this* formulation of them, but from their pre-adoption in popular usage or rational morality or whatever.

One important issue has been sidestepped in this book but should be mentioned. The need for sources of law that will produce rules which are clear, certain, and appropriate will be felt more in some societies than in others, and in some branches of the law than in others. The more other means of social control are invoked the less necessary will be certainty and appropriateness in the law. And it may well be that in a capitalist society the need for certainty is more apparent with regard to commercial law than for family law. I have not measured the extent of the need, but have worked on the assumption that in Western society there is always *some* need for certainty and appropriateness in all branches of the law. In a concrete case one party may be able to benefit from legal ambiguity, but in general it is better for all to be able to know in advance the legal implications of a proposed course of action.

This study is offered as a contribution to the reform of the law. Legal tradition, like other traditions, imposes its own framework of vision. To see the force of the tradition, one must know the tradition and evaluate its impact. To escape from the tyranny of the past one must know the history of the past. To realize how difficult it has been in the past to achieve adequate sources of law is to be put on one's guard against accepting contemporary models of lawmaking as endowed with God-given perfection.

Statements by distinguished authorities about lawmaking frequently contradict one another, and reveal, often unconsciously, the problems in finding the law. As an "appetizer" to this book I offer a few quotations:

"The law is unknown to him that knoweth not the reason thereof and the knowne certaintie of the law is the safetie of all." Edward Coke,

First Part of the Institutes of the Laws of England, (1628), Book 3, Epilogue, 395A.

"But I deny that it is possible for us [i.e., in India] to prefix to our Acts preambles really setting forth the reasons which induce us to pass these Acts. . . . It constantly happens that we agree as to what ought to be done, while we disagree as to the reasons for doing it. . . . I have watched the progress of many important bills through the British Parliament, and I have no hesitation in saying that if it had been necessary to prefix to each of these bills authoritative statements truly setting forth the arguments for what was enacted, none of them could ever have been carried through." *Lord Macaulay's Legislative Minutes,* sel. C. D. Dharker (Madras: Oxford University Press, 1946), pp. 146 f.

"Sur ce principe, il faut s'arêter aux dispositions des Coutumes homologuées, sans s'embarrasser du *pourquoi. Il* suffit qu'elles soient telles qu'on les trouve. *Non omnium quae à majoribus constituta sunt, ratio reddi potest,* JULIANUS 1.22 ff. de Legib. Inde NERATIUS 1. seq. *Rationes eorum quae constituta sunt, inquiri non oportet, alioquin multa, de his quae certa sunt, subverterentur.* Voyez CUYPERS en son *Traité des Procédures Réeles,* Q.117.n.1." ["On this principle one must stop at the provisions of the homologated customs without troubling oneself with the *Why.* "Not for all rules which have been established by our ancestors can a reason be given," JULIANUS, *D.*1.3.20. Then NERATIUS in the next text: "One must not inquire into the reasons for those rules that are established, otherwise many of those that are fixed will be overturned." See CUYPERS in his *Traité des Procédures Réeles,* Q.117.n.1."] G. de Ghewiet, *Institutions du Droit Belgique* (Lille, 1736).

"Compared to the scope of modern law, custom appears to be uncertain in its form and equally indefinite in its application, but quite to the contrary, it made a primitive society rigid in many respects." T. J. Rivers, *Laws of the Alamans and Bavarians,* (Philadelphia: University of Pennsylvania Press, 1977), p. 16.

"La coutume non écrite, qui, par sa souplesse et sa conformité constante avec le voeu des populations, offrait certains avantages, présentait aussi, dans la pratique, d'immenses inconvénients." ["Unwritten custom, which, by its suppleness and constant conformity to the wishes of populations, offered certain advantages, also presented in practice enormous difficulties."] A. Esmein, *Cours élémentaire d'Histoire du Droit français,* 7th ed. (Paris: Sirey, 1906), p. 719.

"Roman law was, in its prime, characterised by a conservatism that resulted in the retention of old forms long after their intrinsic usefulness had disappeared and astute reinterpretation was necessary to make them work in changed social circumstances. Yet, indeed, it is in this that there lies the greatness of the achievement of the Roman jurists and this which makes them a model for every student of jurisprudence: the ability to retain the form while modifying the substance, the mastery of the art of interpretation which effected a harmonising of the opposing claims of justice in the individual case with the certainty that is an essential ingredient of any legal system worthy of the name and the ability to put existing institutions to wholly new uses as new situations developed." J. A. C. Thomas, *Textbook of Roman Law,* (Amsterdam, North Holland, 1976) pp. 5f.

"The work of deciding cases goes on every day in hundreds of courts throughout the land. Any judge, one might suppose, would find it easy to describe the process which he had followed a thousand times and more. Nothing could be further from the truth." B. N. Cardozo, *The Nature of the Judicial Process,* (New Haven: Yale University Press, 1921), p. 9.

"[T]he system of precedents prevents the same question from remaining indefinitely open as the subject of repeated litigation and judicial determination. As early as possible it brings every unsettled question within the scope of a fixed legal principle and takes it out of the sphere of free judicial determination. A judge is bound by the decisions of his predecessors, not because they were necessarily or even presumably wiser than he is—not because their decisions are necessarily or presumably more correct than those at which he would himself arrive—but because it is in the public interest that questions once decided should remain decided." J. W. Salmond in the Introduction to *Science of Legal Method,* by various authors (Modern Legal Philosophy Series, vol. 9; Boston: Boston Book Company, 1917), p. lxxxiii.

"[A]nother abuse of logic . . . consists in the overrefinement of distinctions to a point where the law in its system becomes too esoteric even
for the learned. The case system of law lends itself especially to this
tendency, where distinctions urged by the necessity of counsel have in
some fields reached the point that logical generalization is impossible,
and each case, in effect, in that field, is a general rule of law." Albert
Kokourek, "Editorial Preface," *Science of Legal Method,* p. xlviii, n. 18.

"When confronted with the task of interpreting a statute the accepted
formula is that the judges seek to ascertain the 'intention of the legislature.' " R. W. M. Dias, *Jurisprudence,* 4th ed. (London: Butterworths,
1976), p. 219.

"What about legislation? On the Rating Bill and the Local Government
Bill there was virtually no parliamentary control. These were special-
ist Bills and the Opposition got nothing out of them. On the large Rent
Bill there was rather more genuine discussion. As a result of Opposition
pressure I was able to make a number of improvements in the Bill which
I wanted and which I had been told by the Department or the parliamentary draftsmen were quite impossible. Nevertheless, I agree with
those who say that the Committee Stage as managed at present is an
intolerable waste of time. The Opposition only have a limited number
of objections to make and they pour them all out on the early clauses,
and then they get tired and give in on the later clauses and schedules
which, though they may be very important, are rushed through without
any proper attention.

Of course, I was spoilt by having Jim MacColl. [Joint Parliamentary
Secretary, Ministry of Housing and Local Government]. As a result of
his presence I never bothered to read any of the Bills I got through. I
glanced at them and I read the briefs about them and I also knew the
policies from the White Papers and therefore I knew exactly how the
briefs and the White Papers corresponded with the clauses of the Bills.
But I never bothered to understand the actual clauses, nor did many
Members, not even the spokesman for the Opposition. Both sides worked
off written briefs to an astonishing extent." R. H. S. Crossman, *The
Diaries of a Cabinet Minister* (London: Hamilton and Cape, 1975), vol.
1, 628.

" 'The Law is generally very wise and prudent, Mr. Camperdown; much more so often than are they who attempt to improve it.' " Anthony Trollope, *The Eustace Diamonds*, ch. 28.

Sources of
Law, Legal Change,
and
Ambiguity

I

Sources of Law in Ancient Rome

D.33.6.9.3 (Ulpian 23 *ad Sab.*) When a legacy is left of "father's wine," that alone is legated that the testator regarded as wine, not what his father so regarded. Again, if "wine in the slaves' fund" is legated, the legacy contains what the slaves regarded as wine. Why are the decisions so different? Because the father's wine became for the use of the testator himself; but that in the slaves' fund remained for the use of the slaves. 4. Likewise if "old wine" is legated,
10 (Hermogenian 2 *iuris epit.*) it will be estimated according to the usage of the testator, that is, the number of years that he required for old wine. But if this is not known,
11 (Ulpian 23 *ad Sab.*) that wine is regarded as old which is not new, that is, that even wine of the previous year will be contained in the term "old";
12 (Paul 4 *ad Sab.*) for if another approach was taken what would be considered as the end or the beginning of "old wine"?

By such raising of issues of substantive law, by analysis, and by proffering solutions, the Roman jurists played a leading role in shaping Roman private law which itself has long been regarded as one of the greatest creations of civilization. The evidence is plain that the Romans were greatly interested in substantive private law. The evidence is equally plain that the Romans were relatively very good at making law. In the conditions that then prevailed, juristic doctrine must have been a successful means of law making. But did the Romans, who were so skilled in creating institutions of substantive law, in determining the scope of legal rules, and in drawing fine legal distinctions, pay equal attention to the sources of law? Did they describe accurately the scope of each source of law, did they analyze its authority, and did they strive to make it as efficient as possible? The question may be posed for the Western legal world in general: to what extent is there or has there been concern over making the sources of law as suitable as possible? Are modern legislatures so constituted that they pass clear and satisfactory laws? Do judges set out their judgments in a way that makes the law unambiguous?

The question is particularly important because it would appear that to a very great extent the nature and quality of a source of law affects the growth of the substantive law.[1] Interest in improving substantive law should also be reflected in interest in having satisfactory sources of law.

The starting place for this inquiry is Roman law and in particular the Roman jurists. Legal development through juristic opinion in general offers advantages. A jurist may set out the law or a branch of it systematically, or he may discuss individual legal problems that may have occurred in practice or be, as yet, only theoretical. Above all, the jurist is excellently placed to give arguments for his opinion, to explain its benefits, and, if necessary, defend it from criticism. But legal development by juristic opinion also has disadvantages. In the absence of intervention by legislature, or ruler, or by the courts, there is no clear way of deciding when an opinion is authoritative. If the opinions of jurists conflict, there may be no automatic test for the court to apply in deciding the case. On a very different level is the problem of determining, in the absence of a legislative initiative, by what right jurists acquire the power to make law. Once acquired, this power will naturally tend to continue and even evolve, but something more seems needed for the original acquisition.

For Rome itself the explanation of the original acquisition seems straightforward even in the absence of much direct information. According to the jurist Pomponius writing in the second century A.D., actions and the science of interpreting the laws in early Rome were in the hands of the College of Pontiffs, which in every year appointed one of its members to be in charge of actions of private law.[2] The Roman pontifices did not belong to a special caste of priests, nor did they devote all of their time to religion. Rather, they were men of substance, successful in public life, and until the lex Ogulnia of 300 B.C. they had to be patricians. In all ways, they were close to the men governing the city, and they were a small organized group of men of accepted talent and responsibility. It requires neither great imagination nor a belief that in early Rome religion and law were undifferentiated[3] to understand how it could come about that the power to interpret statute and control legal actions was attributed to them. The steps in the loss of the pontiffs' monopoly of legal interpretation need not detain us,[4] but even afterward, right through even the second century B.C., legal interpretation was basically in the hands of the senatorial aristocracy.[5] The monopoly of those members of the College of Pontiffs who were interested in law was gone, only to be replaced by a factual monopoly of jurists from the same social group as the pontiffs. These jurists might even themselves be pontiffs, witness Quintus Fabius Labeo in 183 B.C., Titus Manlius Torquatus in 170 B.C., Publius Cornelius Scipio Nasica Corculum, Publius Mucius Scaevola *pontifex maximus*, Publius Licinius Crassus Mucianus *pontifex maximus*, Quintus Mucius Scaevola *pontifex maximus*.[6]

In passing it may be noticed that this development provides the explanation to another problem, namely why Roman aristocrats were so interested in giving legal opinions. That the aristocrats might derive social and political prestige and benefit from appearing in court is comprehensible, but not that similar advantages would accrue from interpreting the law. The aristocrats' activity here cannot come simply from their role as patrons: they gave opinions to others as well as to their *clientes*;[7] and in other societies, rather similar in nature, feudal superiors did not see it as their duty to give legal opinions even to their vassals. The explanation is that to be a member of the College of Pontiffs was very desirable for an aristocrat, and to interpret the law was a function of the *pontifices*. Hence, aspirants to the College of Pontiffs would be interested in interpreting law, and the ability to do so would be regarded as a great good. The prestige arising from the act of interpreting remained after the pontiffs' monopoly was broken.

Apart from any laicization of the law this changeover from the College of Pontiffs has a double significance. First, although it may not have been challenged, juristic interpretation had lost any legitimacy it had possessed. Secondly, it had lost its unitary voice. Consequently, despite the great works of the jurists, reliance on juristic opinion brought ambiguity into the law. Under the pontifical monopoly that member chosen to have charge of private actions would speak for the College. Now there was no authoritative way of determining whose view was to be followed. The conflicting views of distinguished jurists are all treated as important. The point is brought out in a number of texts for the republic. In one letter written to his friend and protégé, the jurist Trebatius, Cicero mentions a legal problem involving a certain Silius. Silius had previously consulted Cicero who obtained for him Trebatius's opinion. When he heard this, he told Cicero that Servius and Ofilius had expressed themselves differently, and he asked Cicero to write to Trebatius, as Cicero is now doing, to commend him and his case to the jurist.[8] In a famous case, the *causa Curiana* of around 93 to 91 B.C., Quintus Mucius Scaevola, already mentioned, appeared for one party, and the orator Lucius Licinius Crassus who is praised as a jurist by Cicero for the other,[9] and they offered contrasting interpretations of a will. Cicero also tells us of another conflict of opinion among jurists, this time over the scope of a usufruct of a slave woman. Publius Mucius Scaevola, already mentioned and who was consul in 133 B.C., and Manius Manilius, consul in 149 B.C., held that a child born to the slave woman counted as fruit and therefore belonged to the usufructuary; but Marcus Junius Brutus, praetor in 142 B.C., disagreed. The dispute retained its interest and was referred to, with approval for the view of Brutus that eventually prevailed, by Gaius[10] in the second century A.D. and by Ulpian rather later.[11] We cannot tell how long it took for a consensus to emerge. To the issue of emerging consensus we will return.

A joke in another letter alerts us to a real problem for juristic authority in Roman law. Cicero playfully writes to Trebatius who is campaigning with Caesar:

I very much fear you will freeze during the winter. Therefore I think (and the same was the decision of Mucius and Manilius) that you should make use of a blazing fire, especially since you have no abundance of cloaks.[12]

The humor of the passage lies in Cicero's citing other jurists in support of his trivial recommendation, but there would be no fun in this unless such citation was usual among jurists. And then it becomes important to notice that the supposed arguments of Mucius and Manilius are not given: Cicero simply relies on the authority of the two jurists. Other juristic texts, both inside and outside of Justinian's *Digest*, show that it was in fact common to cite a jurist in support without setting out his reasons. If the reasons of jurists are not reported, one of the great advantages of development by juristic opinion—quality of rules emerging from a weighing of argument—is lost; yet this happening is in part almost inevitable. Particular jurists will come to have a general standing that will weigh in individual situations independently of their arguments. The general standing will be dependent on acceptance by other jurists or on state intervention.

In Rome general acceptance by other jurists was largely based on the status or office of the jurist in the republic and on the office held by the

jurist in the empire, an approach that eventually led to the bureaucratization of law. Also the jurists tended to cite those whose authority was
beyond question, that is, was already firmly established, which naturally
is the case only with older jurists.

We have already seen that the jurists until the end of the second
century B.C. were almost always of senatorial rank and many of the most
famous were pontiffs and also held elected high public office. In the first
century B.C. the *equites* came to the fore,[13] and in the empire it is rare
for a known jurist not to have held an office of state.[14] The leading
jurists of the late classical period were high civil servants: Papinian was
advocatus fisci, assessor to the praetorian prefect, and secretary *a libellis*;[15]
Paul was assessor to Papinian as praetorian prefect, secretary *a memoria*,
and praetorian prefect;[16] Ulpian was also assessor to Papinian as praetorian prefect, probably secretary *a libellis*, *praefectus annonae*, and praetorian prefect.[17] It is against this background that we should set our
knowledge of the jurist, Gaius. It has been stressed that if we take the
evidence at its face value, Gaius was the originator of no less than three
types of legal literature,[18] and the survival rate of texts from his *Institutes*
proves his enormous popularity in legal education. He does not appear
to have held any office or to have been employed in the imperial civil
service. And there is no evidence that he was ever asked for or gave a
responsum, and he is referred to in only one text in the *Digest*.[19] This
neglect by contemporaries and by other Roman jurists is no indication
that his legal ability was considered doubtful: rather his career was not
such as to qualify him to be an authority.

The need for the jurist cited to have authority also explains why
jurists appear to be rather out of date when they cite one another. The
jurist referred to is almost always older, often dead, and seldom up-and-
coming. For instance, Javolenus Priscus who was active in the later first
century A.D. cites jurists by name 205 times; Labeo is the jurist most
often referred to (87 times), and he died between 10 and 21 A.D.; the
jurists of the republic, Trebatius, Ofilius, and Servius come next with
respectively 32, 20, and 14 citations. Of his contemporaries he seems
to cite only the (older) Sabinus 3 times and Longinus twice. Gaius in
his *Institutes* which were written perhaps around 161 A.D. refers most
often to Sabinus, 15 times, and Cassius Longinus (consul in 30 A.D.),
12 times; to the republican jurist Servius 7 times; but to his exception-
ally famous contemporary, Julian, only twice.[20]

Juristic authority was also bolstered by state intervention in the empire in two ways, by the *ius respondendi* and the Law of Citations. For the former we have two basic texts:

D. 1.2.2.49 (Pomponius *sing. enchiridii*). It may be observed in passing that before the time of Augustus the right of delivering replies publicly was not granted by leaders of the state, but persons who had confidence in their own learning gave replies to those who consulted them. Nor did they always give their replies under seal, but often they themselves wrote to the judges, or had those who consulted them testify as to their opinion. The deified Augustus was the first to lay down, in order to give greater authority to the law, that they might give replies on his authority. And from that time this began to be sought as a favor. Therefore, the excellent Emperor Hadrian, when men of praetorian rank sought from him that they might be permitted to give replies, wrote back to them that this was not usually asked for but was simply performed and, therefore, he would be delighted if anyone had faith in himself that he prepare himself for giving replies to the people.[21]

The second text comes from Gaius's account of the sources of law:

G. 1.7 The replies of the jurists are the propositions and opinions of those to whom it is permitted to lay down the law. If the propositions of all of them agree, what they so hold has the force of law. But if they disagree, the judge is permitted to follow whichever opinion he wishes. This is declared by a rescript of the deified Hadrian.[22]

The translation of these texts may be open to doubt, and their general lack of precision has created much dispute as to the meaning of the *ius respondendi*.[23] It does, however, appear from the text of Pomponius that Augustus gave selected jurists the right to utter *responsa* under his authority and seal. Since Augustus was careful not to give himself legislative powers it seems unlikely that he declared these *responsa* legally binding, but in practice they would be very highly persuasive. Nor can we tell whether this *ius publice respondendi* involved giving *responsa* to a judge nor whether all jurists with the right had to be consulted. The reason for the right, according to Pomponius, was to give greater authority to the law, and it would indeed make the opinions of the chosen jurists more authoritative. In addition, the skillful granting of the right could bring legal development by juristic opinion much more under the control of the emperor. Greater precision is not possible for the period, partly because of some confusion in the surrounding fragments of Pomponius. *H. t.* 2.48 seems to say that Sabinus was an *eques* (a knight) and was the first to give *responsa* publicly, and this advantage, once it came to be granted, was given him by Tiberius; and *h. t.* 2.50 repeats that Sabinus was given the right by Tiberius to issue *responsa*. Perhaps the texts mean not that Sabinus was the first jurist to be given the *ius respondendi* but that he was the first *eques* to be so privileged; after all it would be surprising if Augustus had not named anyone after creating the *ius*. If this view is correct, then we have additional point to Pomponius's claim that Augustus's intention was to increase the authority of the law; after a century of legal domination by *equites* and the confusion of long years of civil war, legal authority was to be returned to senatorial jurists.

Hadrian's reform is not clear. Pomponius's account is taken from his one volume of Roman legal history, and it is reasonable to treat his statement as referring to something important rather than to an isolated episode that had no further consequences. It is also reasonable to hold that he and Gaius are concerned with the same rescript.[24] The most obvious interpretation then, I believe, is that Hadrian was simply refusing to make anyone a grant of *ius respondendi*. The *ius* in effect was abolished, with a consequence like that set out in G. 1.7. Only when all influential jurists were agreed was a judge actually bound, because only then was the law settled. It may be relevant here that under Hadrian the *concilium principis* (the emperor's council) became a standing organ of state with permanent salaried members including a number of leading jurists, and imperial rescripts became a major source of law.[25] Other interpretations of Hadrian's activity do exist, but the main significance of the ambiguity here is surely that it reveals how unimportant the *ius respondendi* was. The need to be more specific was not felt. Indeed, Sabinus is the only jurist we know who did have the *ius respondendi*. If Hadrian's reform had made the *ius respondendi* more important, then the grant of the right would mark a decisive step in a jurist's career—just as decisive, though not similar to, receiving a doctorate at a German university or "taking silk" at the English bar—and we would surely expect the event to be recorded for some jurists.[26] A further argument from silence may possibly have some validity. Suetonius, the biographer of the Roman emperors, takes a particular interest in and frequently mentions legal changes for which an emperor is responsible. Yet he does not mention Augustus's introduction of the *ius respondendi*, which is surprising if the innovations had great importance.

The second type of state intervention, that contained in the Valentinian Law of Citations of 426 A.D., was along very different lines:

C. *Th.* 1.4.3 (Emperors Theodosius and Valentinian, Augusti, to the Senate of the City of Rome)
After other matters.

We confirm all the writings of Papinian, Paul, Gaius, Ulpian, and Modestinus so that the same authority attends Gaius as Paul, Ulpian, and the others, and readings from his whole corpus may be cited. We also declare to be ratified the learning of those persons whose treatises and opinions the above-mentioned have incorporated in their own works, such as Scaevola, Sabinus, Julian, and Marcellus, and all whom they cite, provided however they are confirmed, on account of the uncertainty of age, by a collation of the codices. Where different views are produced the greater in number of authors prevails, if the number is equal the authority of that party prevails in which Papinian, man of splendid intellect, shines forth. Just as he overcomes individuals so he yields to two. As was previously enacted, we order to be invalidated the notes of Paul and Ulpian made on the corpus of Papinian. Where their opinions cited in court are equal and their authority is thought to be equal, the decision of the judge decides whom he ought to follow. We order that Paul's sentences also are to be valid. (November 6, 426).[27]

Thus, the constitution made the writings of five classical jurists, Papinian, Paul, Gaius, Ulpian, and Modestinus, primary authorities and also provided for the production of the works of other jurists cited by them. The constitution is often regarded as evidence of the low quality of legal talent in the early fifth century: "Such mechanical treatment of legal authorities shows clearly the low level to which jurisprudence had sunk, and, if it was necessary, justifies the strictures which Theodosius, in the introduction to his Code, passes on the lawyers of his own age."[28] But the Law of Citations tells us nothing about the state of jurisprudence at the time when it was passed; above all, it is not ranking the old, classical, jurists favorably against contemporaries. With the complete bureaucratization of leading jurists came an end to their writing legal

books. Instead they were concerned with the issuing of imperial rescripts and with other official legal business. Changes and advances in
the law were now to be found in the rescripts, and it can scarcely be
doubted that in the main they were the work of jurists and not of the
emperor. But when an issue arose before a court and the opinions of
Papinian, Paul, Gaius, Ulpian, and Modestinus were ranged all on one
side and an imperial rescript was on the other, the latter would prevail.
Any one senior but anonymous postclassical jurist writing in an official
capacity therefore ranked higher than the combined weight of all five
classical primary authorities. The issue addressed by the Law of Citations was rather different. If no rescript relevant to a case could be
found, juristic writing would be treated as valuable, but the old problem
still existed of determining which jurist had the greatest authority. There
is more to the solution of the problem than the no mean virtue of
establishing certainty in the law, though for their achievement here the
originators of the Law of Citations deserve some credit. Notably, Modestinus is included as a primary authority though his current reputation
is not so high as that of others such as Julian, and is also unlikely to
have been so in antiquity. The explanation is that Modestinus, Paul,
Ulpian, and Papinian are the last of the great classical jurists. The aim
of the originators of the Law of Citations, that is to say, was to make
authoritative not so much the best of classical law, but the best of
classical law at its apex, at the end of its development. The inclusion of
Gaius as a primary authority might seem to contradict this, but his
belated fame rested on his *Institutes*. The elementary principles of law
go out of date more slowly than do details.[29]

Thus, the Law of Citations is not giving authority to future opinions
of jurists but is establishing a ranking of past jurists for future cases.
Together with the old *ius respondendi* it represents the sum of official
intervention to determine the weight of juristic authority. This degree
of intervention to achieve *inter alia* certainty may not be much, but it is
greater than any that will appear again for juristic opinions in later
Western tradition.

The texts that we have now looked at, with the addition of
J. 1.2.8—which is the equivalent of G. 1.7—are in effect the totality
of the Roman sources that expressly deal with the status of the authority
of juristic opinion.

One of the main advantages that juristic opinion has as a source of law is the capacity to make continued improvement. The law may be settled but a new view, once suggested, may come to prevail if its superiority is recognized. The unhappy converse is that the law may remain unsettled if there is no consensus among the jurists. This problem may be overcome in various ways. Thus, the rule may be established that the "herrschende Lehre," the dominant opinion, be followed, and usually it will be easy to establish what the dominant opinion is. Or juristic opinion may be used in conjunction with precedent: judges are to take full account of juristic opinion, but a line of judicial decisions is to be treated as binding. Or these two approaches may be combined. The first of these approaches preserves in full the capacity to change the laws when improved opinions emerge. Apart from the *ius respondendi*—which obviously in this regard was not effective—no system developed in Roman law to cope with the problem. In the result many legal questions of great practical significance could and did remain unresolved for centuries. A few examples may be chosen from those that surface in Gaius's *Institutes*, which, it will be recalled, was written around 161 A.D.

To begin with, males were released from *tutela*, guardianship, when they reached puberty: Sabinus and his school required actual physical development to determine this, the Proculians that the youth had completed fourteen years.[30] Justinian settled the dispute in favor of the Proculian view in 529.[31] But the advent of a male's puberty had great practical consequence; until then he could enter a transaction that might injure his patrimony only if he had the authority of his tutor, and he could not make a will at all; moreover, if he had been appointed heir by his father with a clause of pupillary substitution his death before puberty would mean his estate would go not to his heirs on intestacy but to those designated by his father. Difficulties must have arisen in practice: fatherless youths are not exempt from mortality.

Again, on the issue of the validity of a legacy to a person in the power of the heir there were three classical views. The republican Servius held the legacy valid whether conditional or unconditional, but avoided if at the time of vesting the legatee was still in the power of the heir; Sabinus and Cassius held the legacy void if unconditional but valid if conditional; and the Proculians held the legacy void even if conditional.[32] In practice Romans must often have wanted to leave legacies to persons in the power of the heir who would often have been a relative